Mountain.
Memory.
Marsh.

Carol Parris Krauss's *Mountain. Memory. Marsh.* is an open meeting and allows all minutes of gathering to be recorded. Cousin Stan, nature as fourth wall, pandemic apple picking, resisting urge to spy on neighbor in plain sight, tree limbs form cathedrals, focus on peonies during family death, wanting to save a poor stuck animal though realizing it's just a vulture who is perfectly fine. Each poem in this collection feels created by seven lucky cameras pointing everywhere interesting. Anybody who lives in the Mid-Atlantic knows it presents itself like the point nomads from south to north could no longer walk (besides the weather had cooled enough) or nomads from north to south could no longer walk (besides it had not snowed more than two hours). Either way, those travelers planning to keep going decided to rest here and live forever.

—Jeffrey Hecker
author of *Ark Aft*

I was completely captivated from the start by Carol Parris Krauss's new collection *Mountain. Memory. Marsh.* which explores relationships with loved ones and memories but so much more. The second poem in the collection, "Bull Beach as My Mother Goes Blind," is a beautifully constructed tribute to her mother overlaid with a moving eco-poem. Krauss integrates plenty of nature into her work, in fact, offering the reader a transparent glimpse into her upbringing, lifestyle, and values. And with lines like, "To clean / hardwood floors properly, you must get down on your hands / and knees and talk to them" ("Saturday Chores on Greenbrier Road"), it's impossible not to smile. But there is a serious undertone to Krauss's poetry as well. A reader will find this emotive collection both a story that had to be told and a call to pay keen attention to one's own.

—Samantha Terrell
author of *Dismantling Mountains*

Carol Parris Krauss's *Mountain. Memory. Marsh.* lyrically explores the complexities of life and relationships. Woven throughout is evocative imagery of the Mid-Atlantic landscape, but this collection transcends location. Overarching themes of memory, loss, transience, and our inextricable connections to the natural world permeate the poems. Krauss's reverence for the earth anchors meditations on the fleeting nature of existence, as expressed powerfully, for example, in the poem "I think of the Peonies": "How the full flower bends / the thin reed to the ground and then the petals / disappear on the wind. How its glory is its / undoing." In poem after poem, Krauss navigates the emotional terrain of the human experience with empathy, wisdom, and a painter's eye for details.

—Richard Jordan
author of *The Squannacook at Dawn*

Mountain.
Memory.
Marsh.

Carol Parris Krauss

Fernwood
PRESS

Mountain. Memory. Marsh.

©2025 by Carol Parris Krauss

Fernwood Press
Newberg, Oregon
www.fernwoodpress.com

All rights reserved. No part may be reproduced for any commercial purpose by any method without permission in writing from the copyright holder.

Printed in the United States of America

Cover and page design: Mareesa Fawver Moss
Cover image: Dave Hoefler via Unsplash.com
Author photo: Kelly Krauss

ISBN 978 1 59498 182 1

Navigating relationships. Our history. The complexities of life can be similar to the terrain of the Mid-Atlantic. All of the cliches: calm waters, hanging from a cliff. Mother. Brother. Daughter. Friend. Each of these poems uses place to guide the reader through these moments. And possibly reassure them as they navigate the switchbacks, enjoy the quiet of lavender fields, and watch the marshlands slowly disappear. Proof to readers that they are not alone as they travel this journey through Mountain. Memory. Marsh.

Contents

Acknowledgments 13
Pretty Bottles All in a Row 15
Bull Beach as My Mother Goes Blind 16
The Texture of the Heart 17
Pickett's Tomb, Hollywood Cemetery,
    Richmond, Virginia 18
What He Heard in Leavenworth 19
When the Fairies Take Residence for Winter 20
When I Tell You This, I Lie 21
Apple Picking During Covid 22
Charon Stops by Cedar Grove Cemetery 23
Where the Fairies Frolic 24
My Back to the Fescue 25
Saturday Chores on Greenbrier Road 26
If It's Not Broken 27
A Gwynn Island Blessing for a Fair Sail 28
I cannot take a lover, ... 29
We Long for Broken Waters and Full Sails 30

Beware of Strangers Bearing Gifts in the Garden	31
He was an out-of-work snake preacher.	32
Breaking and Entering	34
Flailing	35
Norfolk Greets Lord Dunmore	36
the ruts of highway 58	37
Like the *Mary Celeste*	38
I Think of the Peonies	39
This Neighborhood	40
When I Build My Snow Globe	41
Molting to More	42
The Hurricane	43
Port Haywood	44
What You Fail to See from Your Kitchen Window	45
The Ghost Forest	46
Neap tide	47
Ashes to Ashes	48
I Learned Silence	49
The Ash-Freckled Snow	50
My Daughter	51
Cousin Stan Steals	52
Brother's Log Cabin and Equine	53
Saint Somebody Deep in Appalachia	54
She Holds Book to Belly	55
Winter Waits	56
Guardrails and Armrests	57
The Rails We Ride	58
Another Hiker Lost in the Woods	59
There is nothing more graceful than the passage of a pregnant lady.	60
Signs	61
Daddy's Home	62
Plum Point Park	63

Trails and Treks of West Ghent 64
Dismal Swamp @ Dusk 65
No Magnolia Wreaths 66
I Come from a Long Line of Storytellers 67

Title Index 69
First Line Index 73

Acknowledgments

"Pretty Bottles All in a Row": *One Art*
"Bull Beach as My Mother Goes Blind": *Winner of Eastern Shore Writers Crossroads Competition*
"The Texture of the Heart": *Amsterdam Quarterly*
"Charon Stops by Cedar Grove Cemetery": *Bay to Ocean Anthology, 2021*
"Where the Fairies Frolic": *Green Ink*
"My Back to the Fescue": *The Broadkill Review*
"Sunday Chores on Greenbrier Road": *Anti-Heroin Chic*
"If It's Not Broken": *Anti-Heroin Chic*
"A Gwynn Island Blessing for a Fair Sail": *Poetry Society of Virginia/Colonial Piecemakers Quilt Guild Exhibit Selection*
"We Long for Broken Waters and Full Sails": *Bay to Ocean Anthology, 2021*
"He was an out-of-work snake preacher.": *The Bear Creek Gazette*
"Norfolk Greets Lord Dunmore": *Norfolk Arts Pavement Poet Selection*
"The ruts of Highway 58": *Plainsongs Poetry Magazine*
"I think of the peonies": *Mixed Mag*

"This Neighborhood": *Pax Morrigan*
"When I Build My Snow Globe": *Black Bough Christmas and Winter Edition, 2021*
"Pickett's Tomb": *Poetry Society of Virginia Anthology 2022*
"The Rails We Ride": *The Dead Mule School of Southern Literature*
"Plum Point": *Elizabeth River Trails 2022 Poem Project*
"Cousin Stan Steals": *Bay to Ocean Anthology, 2022*
"What You Fail to See From Your Kitchen Window": *Susurrus*
"The Hurricane": *North Carolina Bards Anthology 2022*
"When I Tell You This, I Lie": *Pine Mountain Sand & Gravel: The Strange, Stranger, and Estranged Side of Appalachia.*
"Dismal Swamp @ Dusk": *Does it have Pockets*
"I Come from a Long Line of Storytellers": *december magazine*

Some of these poems appeared in the chapbook *Just a Spit Down the Road* (Kelsay, 2021) and the chapbook The Old Folks Call it God's Country (The Poetry Box, 2024 Spring).

Pretty Bottles All in a Row

My grandparents' home was thumb-smashed
into the side of a mountain. The garage
a dark cave with drills, hammers, and chains
crisscrossing from the rafters. Above it was
a wide porch. A swing at one end and a slider
covered in cabbage-rose vinyl at the other end.
It would squeak and rustle simultaneously
when propelled by your feet.

My family would pile into our Pontiac station wagon and traverse
Caesars Head to spend afternoons with my father's parents.
After Papaw passed, they told me he was an alcoholic.
I don't remember that. I do recall a chest filled
with carved wooden toys, his ability to tell a tale,
and his laugh. Half-Camel unfiltered.
Half bubbling mountain stream.

I also recollect all those pretty bottles on the kitchen window ledge.
Some slender, others rotund or just plain squatty. Bright blue,
ruby red. Gulf green. The sun would hit them right around noon.
Each bottle glistened. Throwing a rainbow against the kitchen walls.
Painted, covered what this grandchild didn't know.
Didn't want to know.

Bull Beach as My Mother Goes Blind

She says the new drops sting, the magnifying glass is no help, and she can no longer see the large-print Bible. The doctors have no remedy. The time will come when the light will crumble. Dark will sweep across Mother's eyes and claim her vision.

They say Poquoson, bound by water on three sides, will erode hundreds of feet in the next thirty years. Bull Beach has been rattled and tattered by tidal winds, hurricanes, and contrary currents.

She says the light in the living room is bad. High ceilings and low windows cast shadows on *The Times* as she strains to read the obituaries. Seeking names she knows.

They say the elements are eating the land where cattle once roamed among the marshes. Poquoson is being scrubbed from the Peninsula. Eaten away by its own.

She says the fluorescent kitchen lights are too harsh, and the humming is a distraction. The cat sits under her chair, catches the crumbs that fall from her fork. A fork she can't see properly due to the glare's blurred reflections.

They say a plan will only slow the bay, Wythe Creek, and Back River invasion. Dredging, sand dunes, and new vegetation are merely bandaids. The time will come when the stilted houses will crumble. Sand will sweep cottage porches, and the sea will claim the land.

The Texture of the Heart

If you peel back the pericardium, snap the thick sac, tear
the heart from the ligaments binding it to the spinal cord
and diaphragm, lift the pulsing machine in your hand, and move
to the light for closer inspection, would you find that the fabric
of the heart is parallel to the texture of the owner's personality?

Would Mother be a sensible calico, Father burlap knobby-like tree bark,
sister cords of corduroy discontent, and the lone duck who sits
in my front yard without his mate, the one he has proudly waddled
around with for a month, his plump, mottled gold beauty,
who has suddenly gone missing, would his heart be shredded satin
similar to the material that lines a coffin and blankets a lifeless body?

Or if you peel back the pericardium, snap the thick sac, tear
the heart from the ligaments binding it to the spinal cord
and diaphragm, lift the pulsing machine in your hand, and move
to the light for closer inspection, would you find that you have
simply stopped the heart from beating, and it suddenly sits smooth
like the satin grass the lonely male duck rests in, waiting for his
missing mate?

Pickett's Tomb, Hollywood Cemetery, Richmond, Virginia

Dogwoods stood sentry under the Union blue sky.
Leaned over the carriage paths, war widows
prostrate in mourning. Lace petticoats.

General George Pickett's tombstone stood at the end
of a lane on the cemetery's edge. Circular, solitary.
The clatter of cars crossing Robert E. Lee Bridge

and James River rushes and ramblings,
the only accolades accompanying Pickett in death.
Dirges more palatable than the drops of liquor

that had slowly killed him. Steady sips of pity. Shame.

What He Heard in Leavenworth

Night after night, cockroaches roam the floors. Guys shuffle around a lot. Vick witnesses certain things—"things that should stay in prison," he will later say, refusing to comment further—that disturb him too much to sleep. At first, he tries earplugs. Then he applies for a midnight-shift job, mopping floors for 12 cents an hour.
　—Seth Wickersham, ESPN

They honored him at halftime. On the same emerald field
where cadets trooped in a cloud of white. Tech fans
cheered him. Shook their key chains in delight. Honored
this man. The same Hokie star who spent twenty months
in Leavenworth mopping floors at night. Paid twelve cents
an hour. Imprisoned, he heard howls he declared no one
should ever hear. Shrieks, snarls, ripping flesh. Pain
that should remain in his minimum-security camp
located in the middle of the verdant fields of Kansas. Noises
not for cheerleaders, fans of football, or ordinary folk.
Maybe he heard the exact same sounds that sentenced him
to pass daytime in Leavenworth playing chess and nighttime
confined, covering his ears.

When the Fairies Take Residence for Winter

The fairies in the field have moved to the attic. The frost-tipped nettle and ice-bent boughs have turned them toward the heat of the hearth. They have donned socks of finest Aran wool and, from the sounds of it, play slide, hide, and seek among the boxes, tag with daddy longlegs. I hear the flutter of their wings against the rafters and the twitter of their laughter. I long to pull the trapdoor and join the herd. They will reside until May taps at the dormer window crooks, a command reminding them to begin. To commence to stitch the corners of the fairy ring and embroider the bonnet of the early crocus.

When I Tell You This, I Lie

I tell you that I sometimes see a flash of a slick segmented tail
    as I roundthe steps. Grab the mahogany banister
    like hundreds of people before me.

I tell you that I can hear clicking as it slides between the walls.
    Among pipes and Pepto-Bismol pink insulation,
    something lives.

When I tell you that I am not alone when I make my late-night
    trip to the bathroom. Hear hurried scurry just before
    I fumble and flip the light switch.

When working the garden, eradicating the Virginia buttonweed,
    I can hear wails and hissing pouring
    from the slats of the house eaves.

That my neatly hung skirts, pressed shirts, and creased pants
    jerk on the windless air. Jump off of the hangers.

I tell you that as I read, with my back against
    Great Aunt Martha's antique bed, from behind
    the headboard, I feel a moist breath upon my neck.

When I tell you that exterminator after exterminator
    inspected the house with no discoveries. No lairs,
    no nests. All clear, time after time.

I tell you that I can have cookies for dinner, no less. That I enjoy
    the solitude and that sharing is overrated.
    One in a double bed.

    When I tell you there is nothing worse than growing old
        alone. When I tell you this, I lie.

Apple Picking During Covid

We paid our fare at the bottom gate
    palmed our hand-drawn entry ticket.
A dirt road peeled and spiraled
    Carter's apple orchard. Trees leaned
into our car window, and open palms
    offered their fruit. Reds, pinks, and almost
orange orbs. Bees dotted and darted among the
    crooked branches as they pulled their shift.
At the peak leaned a barn laden with apple
    offerings. Cider. Jam. Pies. There our boot
was loaded with a basket of fragrance, glory,
    and desire by a man in a dusty, worn mask
and juice-stained overalls. Working his old world
    in a new way. One changed by an
apple-colored contagion, shaped like fruit no one
    is tempted to want. No Red Delicious.

Charon Stops by Cedar Grove Cemetery

Three streets over, at the sea-foam green ranch, the family car
is a hearse with flame flanks and oversized tires. The orange

side-window curtains have tassels which sway when
the funeral coach traverses the bridge to Churchland.
Affixed to the bumper is a peace sign

decal and a Be Nice sticker. I once saw the driver,
a middle-aged man with a receding hairline and followed
his hearse, my one-woman processional.

Modern-day Charon went about his weekly errands
to the dry cleaners, the local library with the scummy
lily pond in the front, and then a quick drop-off

at the Goodwill drive-up. A chauffeur willing to drive death,
to call shotgun as he made his last stop at the Cedar Grove
Cemetery on Effingham Street.

Placed flowers on a grave and reminded death who was piloting
this hearse and who wasn't.

Where the Fairies Frolic

I have heard tales of bluebell woods
where fairies scamper to slip and slide
after moon puts sun to bed.

Down endless lapis petals
and waves of crisp waters of canopy,
they frolic until weary and worn.

To then sip a nightcap
of a lavender elixir
and crawl into cowslip.

Shutter the nodding yellow clusters
as sun bosses moon away
for another day.

My Back to the Fescue

Again, I am ten. My
back to the fescue,
bumblebees, and no-see-ums
looping around my head.
Aerobatic insects.

At the edge of the water is dog,
mud socks and dripping burnished
locks of a Setter.

I hold my right arm high, make
a pencil of my index finger and thumb.
Trace the lion, bear, and elephant
in the sky.

A mockingbird calls, and the willow
sapling bends to gulp Lake Norman.
I outline the giraffe and alligator
clouds as they meander across the sky/////.

A cumulus circus ambling through my
childhood. The dogs, the birds, a tree
with no backbone to witness. My story
penned in the sky.

Saturday Chores on Greenbrier Road

My mother will tell you. And my grandmother, too. To clean
hardwood floors properly, you must get down on your hands
and knees and talk to them. You must counsel the gouge
in the living room, you need to comfort the water stain
by the back door. Gently coax and whisper out the flour, sugar,
and holiday crumbs near the bottom edges of the oven.
You need to soap, scrub, and oil these eighty-two-year-old planks.
Each slab of timber will listen to you. Each tongue, groove,
and peg will hear your psalm of work on this cool winter morning.
It will take hours to complete this ritual, and you will feel
the aches in your hips, knees, and wrists tomorrow.
Your body will talk to you. The language of your
hardwood floors.

If It's Not Broken

I have taken her items that are chipped, torn, water-stained. I did not take the gold earrings but instead the cracked mirror. The one Granny used when she would brush, twist, and secure her auburn hair with a tortoise comb. I want the broken necklaces, always the chipped china. The silver letter holder that sat on the edge of her splintered desk. Patina-tipped, dented. I can slide my memories neatly in the slots, like how Granny would turn her head toward her shoulder and tilt the mirror just so to inspect her fixed hair. Right before smoothing the snag on her skirt, she called me to her lap for an hour of flawless story time. Our perfect ritual.

A Gwynn Island Blessing for a Fair Sail

A long weekend in a cracked cottage leaning
  on the Middle Peninsula edge.   We pushed
    kayaks to the bay. Slipped the clove-hitch
shore, coasted beyond the grasp and hue
  of the blue crab. A scrub-and-oyster-shell
    shore at our backs. Knotty pines to knobby spines.
Bound by the Rappahannock and Piankatank Rivers,
       this neck is hailed as the *Boating Capital of the Chesapeake Bay*.
I don't know about that or know the flow and   cast of these waters.

   I do know as our neon-colored envelopes
slipped the cleats of Deltaville dirt, bobbled and balanced
gentle waves, and drifted
  toward the horizon, I didn't hear or   see large yachts.
No rhythmic engine
    purr. No tourist laughter cresting in my direction as they
sunned on deck. I simply spied the tip fin of the Sandbar shark,
accepted a Gwynn's Island blessing   for a fair sail.

I cannot take a lover,

for the right side of the bed, given to me by Great Aunt Martha, is broken. I never met Great Aunt Martha, the aunt to Aunt Nancy, the wife of Uncle June, the lone brother to my mother.

She must have known the bed was faulty, why else would a sensible Appalachian Mountain woman gift a bed to a relative of a relative she had never met. The narrow lip, upon which the bed slat should rest snuggly, has dried and splintered. The nails pulled from the wood— rusty, bent. Useless.

The right side of the bed is now supported by an old suitcase, complete with travel stickers and a piece of plyboard extended by two screws. Phillips. Arms reaching, fingers grasping to just touch the splintered lip where the bed slat should tightly fit. The right side of the bed will support nothing more than my ten-pound dowager dachshund,

so I cannot take a lover.

We Long for Broken Waters and Full Sails

Sailboats tight with anchors resist the change of tide like the broken hand on Daddy's pocket watch, the fox nesting, the bird on a branch. Landlocked.

Colder tonight but still sleeting, the needles pinging the front window mute the barks of tug boats and naval ships. The lanterns on the Monitor-Merrimac Bridge, barely seen, stand regardless with circles, dreams of billowing sails and open seas, a light of hope around a city.
Locked.

Nautical charts mark the shoals, the shallows, the cuts to the bay, the open-mouthed Atlantic. Yet we sit upon a billet of safety one year into a storm. Blight. Round and blurred like the lights on the Monitor-Merrimac Bridge. Moored, waiting to be cast untethered to open seas. Longing for days of sails full. The bridge's beacons and Norfolk's broken waters far behind us.
Unlocked.

Beware of Strangers Bearing Gifts in the Garden

I have seen the silver rabbit three times now,
he is plump with exclamation-mark ears.
Partial to the twisted hedge by the fence,
he nests and rests into monkey-grass pallets.

I leave vegetable scrap tokens—
head of carrots, lettuce, and onion
cells for him. I have dubbed him Oliver
and whistle into the winter dark for him
to come visit with me. To sit and chat
at the garden bench.

I receive no return answer from Oliver,
only an inky indigo the witching-hour
throws back at me. His mother's quiet
warning to beware of strangers bearing
gifts in the garden.

He was an out-of-work snake preacher.

Owned one dead snake and one with a nasty boil directly above his rattler. His wood-trimmed station wagon, which he affectionately called Zeus, had expired and rested rusty under a Cypress tree. A tattered briefcase sat on the TV tray located to the left of the portrait of Jesus. The case was a faux-leather vessel filled with empty and unanswered prayers and pleas. He blamed that little girl from Pumpsville.

He banged the cracked and tape-repaired remote on the side of his recliner and flipped channels until he found Preacher Joel. He could have been famous with a comely wife and slicked-back hair. Pearly whites. Beady eyes in front of millions of people. The girl had twitched and foamed. Some thought she had been overcome with the Holy Spirit. Joel's offering plates were teeming with bills and checks.

Rasmus, the ornery rattler, watched the TV sermon. Flicked his tongue at his oozing, inflamed boil. His aquarium sat by the front door, and the sun painted a halo on his triangular head. Then her legs had shot straight up, and her lace petticoat spread around her prone body. The bottom of her Mary Jane shoes were scuffed, and one had a penny-sized hole in it.

Swanson makes a mean spaghetti dinner, which our out-of-work rattler reverend had ingested before the sermon. He was now belching garlic and Coca-Cola to "When the Saints Come Marching In." There weren't too many traveling serpent preachers left. A dying breed. Doc Kyle had come over from Bear Creek to tend to the child. He was too late. Rasmus had already crawled back into his case. Curled up and was taking a snooze.

Archie Bunker would follow Preacher Joel on Channel 3. Now there was a good man. One who knew who he was and where he was going. He sure showed Edith. Reverend reptile had sprinted out of that church and scooped up the dollar and change offerings by the vestibule. Managed one last run out of Zeus. Sand was spitting and tires were screeching. I'm not saying she was the last nail in his career, but I am saying he was the last nail in her pink and pearly white coffin.

Breaking and Entering

I stand on the HVAC unit outside the bedroom window, pull
up on the window frame, and belly scooch across the sill.
It is dark, and someone in the house is gently snoring.

I fold and unfold each leg into the room. Sit for a minute
on the quilt of pale-yellow roses, careful not to disturb
the occupant.

I then expand and fill the room with all of my mind, wisdom,
and spring of azalea, dandelion, crabgrass, apple blossom,
and wisteria.

I hear the click of the front door and pull back the blinds
to see Winter's back as he moves down the front walkway.
And just like that, I have arrived.

Flailing

Down Greenbrier Street, a block before the estuary,
trees cathedral over the blacktop. A ribbed vault.

From the gray of my sedan, I notice something flailing
yet very much alive, a shadow in an oil-slicked pothole.

Slowing down with aspirations of saving a trapped
duck, a small bunny, or the neighbor's calico, I stop

and prepare for the rescue. Grab a beach towel
from the back seat and a flashlight from the glove box.

As I step out of my car, a buzzard unfurls his wings.
Stares me down and then lifts from the road

into the early night sky. A duck, bunny, or the
neighbor's calico gripped tightly in his talons.

Flailing.

Norfolk Greets Lord Dunmore

Listen for the bells of old St. Paul.
Spared a torching in 1738 but marked
by a cannonball in her south wall.

the ruts of highway 58

the trees were not blurred. each distinct. the knot holes, broken limbs, crumbling bark on the oak, and the ruddy laced maple. i saw her weave among the trees, her skirt dragging mud spits, snagging on briars, and evading berry-tipped fingernails. she danced among the fog and mist of dismal swamp, and i watched her from the back-seat window. i wasn't surprised to see her. i wasn't surprised she was trailing after my car. she had been running recon on me for fifty-eight years. whispers, shoulder taps, checks at the tracks before whistle warnings. that time on the trestle when i slipped on slick moss and boone's farm. netted me from plummeting into the french broad river currents and swirls. it was her boldness that surprised me. her threshold from my mind to running sentry. sentry among the wraith militia of the revolutionary and civil wars that surprised me. forest haints. i pressed my face to the cold pane and envisioned her jumping tombstones, broken sabers, and rattletrap cannons to ride me home as the nor-easterner bore down, pushed the car with fists of wind. swiped the car to the edge of the road, where she simply held up her palms and, with a flick of power, guided the nissan back into the ruts of highway 58. wiped her hands on her white petticoat and glided behind a pine.

Like the *Mary Celeste*

Will it be like the *Flying Dutchman* or maybe the *Mary Celeste*
with cobwebbed china, rickety railings, and a table set
of fine china and patina silver? A state of arrested decay.
Or will it be more like Bodine? Dusty saloons, cat houses,
and hitching posts? A ghost hitch. Abandoned mines. Hundreds
of years from now, will a stranger wander into my classroom,
see the date 3/13/2020, Friday the 13th, on the right-hand corner
of the board in perfect teacher script, and wonder what caused
this room to be abandoned? Will explorers see the rotten apple
on my desk, the ungraded essays, and the set of dog-eared novels
on the rickety shelf and imagine the worst? National Geographic
may find thousands of similar rooms dotted across the world
and film a documentary. An exploration into abandoned minds.
A study of the education system before the pandemic. A movie
ending with a broken strip of film flapping against a projector.
An exposé on arrested development in the year 2020.

I Think of the Peonies

I think of the peonies. Not the unplugging of monitors and alerts, the white rose on the hospital door, the silent buzz. Not the tears trickling down his face. How he held my daughter's hand as she combed his hair and moistened his cracked lips. Not his last moment of coherence, when he sternly read us a to-do list. Not how he gave us passwords and account numbers. Not the burial. The overflowing crowd who honored him. But I think of how the peony bloom stays tight like a child's fist and then, in seconds, bursts into full bloom. How the stem is simply too slender to hold the full weight of the blossoms for any length of time. How the full flower bends the thin reed to the ground, and then the petals disappear on the wind. How its glory is its undoing. I think of the peonies.

This Neighborhood

This neighborhood. The dog behind us barks in frustration at his fence, another mutt two streets over answers him. A wrench clanking on the driveway and the thud of a skateboard as it moves from sidewalk to street. Three boys on bikes scream in unison as they go no feet, no hands for as long as the bikes will coast. A belch of a tugboat as it rounds the curve of the estuary and the buzz of an ATV filled with teenagers in dripping swimsuits. Gilly, the house cat, chatters as a squirrel taunts him from the front tree. Thirty seconds. A snapshot. This neighborhood.

When I Build My Snow Globe

In my snow globe, I will position Dad in his recliner.
We will gather in the den with Daniel, distributing gifts,
Kelly crisscross on the floor by the fireplace,
and the great-grandkids running ribbons among the dogs,
Rags the cat, and a mess of wrapping paper. After the season
all but Dad will resume their daily routines.
I will wrap him in glitter-sprinkled tissue. Nestle
and gently store him among other family treasures.

Molting to More

We long to be more than just another tourist, what the locals call
a *Come-Here*. Escape from work, bustle, obligations rooted to land
each chance we can. Stow the dock shoes, puppy, and bare basics

into the car. Head to the north and then east toward the Chesapeake's
fingertips. Each of us needs the water for a different purpose. Hears
a call to dip our toes in baptismal waters. Speak of someday.

The time when we live in our stilted cabin with wide, worn plank floors,
walk to the end of our pier to pull up our crab pots, become a familiar face
at Richardson's Cafe after Sunday service.

Shed the *Come-Here* like a soft-shell crab
molting at the first kiss of spring.

The Hurricane

It storms the coast, rears back its head, and roars. Sour-breath
fog. Pulls its body to the sand dunes, shreds the eelgrass.

Tosses the turtle nests. Cleaves the blacktop and eviscerates
the belly of town. Main Street Drug Store. The courthouse. The diner.

Gathers prey in sharp yellow teeth and shakes its head.
A spiked tail thrashes stilted cottages. Flings screened doors.

With time, it wears itself out and retreats to the waters.
Sated. The tempest slides in a bed littered with pages

from books, diaries, love letters. Flotsam. Untethered photos
of weddings, graduations, and baby's first dip in the ocean.

Port Haywood

The paths of the water, jagged incomplete jigsaw puzzles. Harbors,

inlets, dark backwaters. Home, a Port Haywood houseboat for four

days. Four a.m each day, the roar of watermen vessels as they

cast off to tend crab pots, throw nets to the maw of the bay.

We tossed quilts and stumbled to the makeshift porch to sip

coffee and watch the sun clamber to the sky. At the edge of

paradise, we counted. Oysters briny and piquant, shrimp

dipped in butter and lemon spray, blessings flowing

through our hands. Unable to root for as long

as we want. Quick, elusive like waves

returning to the waters.

What You Fail to See from Your Kitchen Window

I have spoken of Deltaville. How we cast off our kayaks,
wiggled into the Chesapeake like water worms. Sotted Ssssses
as we balanced to right our craft, to take purchase.

Soon slicing the water as we traversed down a nooked cove.
Then, lifting our oars and letting only the wind and kelpies steer us
past a ring-billed gull, a red hound sunning at the frayed blue-gray edge.

You may have spied us from your ramshackle dock
or cottage porch. Wondered what fools would trust the bay
to nothing but the wind. Oars out, mother and daughter drifting.

To you who pruned your coneflowers, unfolded from weeding
to wave to us frantically, we knew what we were doing. A pair
of mountain women curled up in kayaks, looking at the sun

spit-polishing the water. Worshipping your slice of the Chesapeake Bay.
Relishing all you fail to see from your kitchen window.

The Ghost Forest

The marsh will walk. Stomp right

up to the pine forest and attack.

Sand wave after sand wave forces.

Saltgrass ambushing whatever gets

in the way. Watermen haints watching

from pungys. See modern man undoing

what nature scripted and etched long ago.

Neap tide,

the couple walks the fringe
    of the Atlantic. Stops to scoop sand, sift, and waterfall
between fingers. Looking for treasures. Welks. Moon shells.
Their dog, a spaniel of some kind, wanders
    among the saltmeadow cordgrass. Noses the carcass
of a ghost crab.

I watch
    from the cottage's front porch. My eyes moving
    from couple to dog and back again.

I have watched so long. The tide, the tourists.
Different dogs. Different couples. Some with children, instead.
Some alone. One. Many.

Mesmerized by the invisible threads that bind us
and then snap
    as they move beyond my vision. Taking shells
while I create names, stories for each of them. Wonder
where they are from, what brought them to my backyard water.

    Then leaving. Only footprints evidence. Soon to be washed
as the next tide creeps closer to my cottage. As I watch.

Ashes to Ashes

They say the snow will begin just after one.
Our bellies will be full, and football streaming
on the television. We will take turns stepping
out the back door, looking to the sky, and holding
up our palms. Once the snow begins and the flakes
become quarter-sized, we will dress the puppy in her sweater,
gear up in parkas and boots, and walk to the end of the street.
A bench at the water's edge calls to us. We sip wine from a thermos,
watch the puppy chase flakes. As dark approaches, we will turn
to come home. Look over our shoulders one last time to see the wind
scuttle snow through the bridge's belly. Watch it smack the pilings,
drop into the water. Back from where it came. Ashes to ashes.
Dust to dust.

I Learned Silence

I learned silence like braille, feeling the bumps.
Tracing the sharp edges of once broken limbs.

All I really wanted was to gush forth
like Crabtree Falls. An endless

stream of objections, rejections. Opinions
coursing over slick stones, climbing the edges

of the riverbank. Overflowing into the copse
of frail young loblollies. Covering the spring moss

and lifting dead and dried leaves like bruises
coming into their purples and blues.

The ones on the arms and wrists of a girl
who learned silence all too well.

The Ash-Freckled Snow

Two teenagers play in the ash-freckled snow,
    pine trees and shadows, a tent

shading their footsteps, where they came from,
    where they reside.

At first glance, I only see the taller one,
    bending and folding like the crane repairing the naval ship

in Norfolk harbor, sculpting snowballs.
    Sometimes stopping to hurl a misshapen missile at the other.

That one on the ground, making angels. Motions
    like my rusty kitchen scissors.

Bright parkas and mismatched gloves, one with a fluff-topped
    toboggan. They play in the street

for close to an hour. Then gather themselves and head toward
    the estuary cottages. That awkward head down,

shoulder-dipped shuffle of a teenager. The gait of one torn
    between finishing their shipyard job application

or playing one more hour in the ash-freckled snow.

My Daughter

My daughter is a storm with bones of wind
wrapped in skin. She is static, vibrating from toe
to top. Hair blown and whipping.

My daughter is a nor-easterner rolling
in from the horizon. She is the eye of the storm
too.

The still right before she thrashes her hands,
stomps her feet. Wipes out cities. Retires
her name.

Cousin Stan Steals

They stare at me as they slice their slab of Easter ham
or settle into the couch to watch the Clemson game. They
wonder where they will next find themselves. In stanza three
or maybe the title. Possibly a limerick about the time they
covered me, just a newborn napping in my crib, in stuffed animals.
My siblings. They are onto me. My niece and nephews too.
Tired of reading about how Daniel has the biggest heart. Mom
isn't sure how she feels about me lamenting her loss
of vision or my profound and quite public mourning of my father.
How he appears in every other poem. It's a tad too much.
Being that we are a chin-up, buttoned-down family. Still, I
watch. Watch cousin Stan steal the cookies, all of them, from my
father's funeral reception. Aluminum foil sticking out of his
suit pocket. I wait at least five minutes before heading to the church
restroom to take out my pen and place him on line seven.

Brother's Log Cabin and Equine

They both lorried up to the fence. One bay, the other a pinto.
Dainty steps among the slurry, flanks twitching from Breeze's fly bites.
Tentative but still curious, their muzzles quivered as we
delivered forehead and poll scratches. They took our carrot
and apple slice offerings. Munched while a calico wove stitches
through their feet, nuzzled fetlocks. The two turned in unison.
Unspoken. Gave us their gaskin and galloped to the far fence line.
Stopped just short of the barbed wire to nibble orchardgrass.

We watched a short while. Unspoken, we pivoted. Hand in hand,
ambling to the screened porch. A mother and daughter, more city
than country, perched on the lip of Brother's log cabin. Exploring.
Enjoying what falls beyond our comprehension. Drops into the space
between our clasped hands.

Saint Somebody Deep in Appalachia

She stands near to two feet, one palm reaching out in surrender.
The other hand jagged and broken off at the wrist. Saint Somebody.
Her gown pleat cracks, and ivy strands infested with veins of spider
sacs lace her sandals. Today all the Pignut hickory leaves are black,
and the sky is charcoal detritus.

She stands watch over a parched pond with circular lesions.
Behind her in the umbra of Hammick Hill, a prayer bench is
sanctified in coal ash. Only the pedestal for the wooden cross
remains with stained-glass boards and a heavy lock,
the chapel's solitary congregation.

She stands deep in the trough of a ripped-up mountain range.
Gutted. She should be shedding tears, but her ducts
are clogged with greed. One eyeball crumbled clean
from its socket. Saint Somebody can't even see
clearly enough to walk the Stations.
Offer up a Missa defunctorum.

She Holds Book to Belly

The occupants of the peach-colored Cape Cod sitting catty-corner

to our home have plopped a recliner in the middle of their backyard.

A bright plaid fabric. The daughter of the house has settled

in and popped the footrest. She holds a book to belly and

appears to be sipping a Mason jar concoction. The sun

coats her face, and I hear humming. I watch

from the reading chair beside my front window.

Mind you, I am not spying. Nor am I judging.

In fact, after I finish reading the next chapter

of my book, I plan on locating my sewing box from deep

within the linen closet, pulling out the yardstick and

measuring the width and depth of my chair to ensure

it will pass through my kitchen door.

Detours from destinations.

Winter Waits

Winter waits. To devour. Feed on the unsuspecting.

The youngest child taking out the rubbish at twilight,

Ruff Ruff let loose to relieve himself by the back hedge,

Father running to the store for milk and bread. None

aware of what stands quietly behind them, crouches

in the shadows by the shed, stretches low in the backseat

of the car. Hungry.

Simply waiting.

Guardrails and Armrests

Our car left the valley, began to climb the mountains.
Traversed tunnels chiseled deep in the mouth of the massif.
Too scared to peer over the guard rail.
Too frightened to look up at the endless range.

I held tight to my armrest. Sang my silly song of comfort.
A lullaby from my ancestors. Aliens, folk who came before me
and mine.

Impoverished French-Irish who climbed this cordillera with nothing
more than cloth-clad feet and injudicious guts. No armrest,
no safety rail.

Two steps from free-falling and unfathomable footsteps from
a new life. Miles before they could rest.
Contrive their song of comfort in this remote world
of granite giants.

The Rails We Ride

Steel stitching nearly across the back stoop step.

A 2:00 a.m. and 6:00 p.m. *Southern Rail* snake jounced

the dishes in Granny's hutch, hopped the kitchen-table chairs

clear to the living room. Smoke-steamed the patchwork curtains,

and a long wail startled the baby. Twice daily without fail.

For three years, the rattle and rail trailed me as I washed floors,

changed dirty diapers. Every Saturday, wiped down walls

dotted in cabbage-rose wallpaper. Thin as shoebox cardboard.

Wondered what would happen if I removed my apron, asked Tina

from next door to babysit.

Didn't even scratch out a hasty goodbye. Just grabbed that rusty

caboose ladder. Felt my legs swing out and take purchase on nothing

but danger. Become a passenger instead of a witness.

Another Hiker Lost in the Woods

Roots. Bones. Both gnarled, white. Grasping
at ankles, legs. The hiker lost in the throat
of the woods. The one running from the rustle
behind the boscage. Breaths. Hot, moist
upon his neck. Ragged. He zigs and zags.
Never notices the shadow standing
before him. The end of the trail.

There is nothing more graceful than the passage of a pregnant lady.
The lists to and fro. Ballasts shifting. Cargo—
  Saffron
        Asafoetida
               Sumac
                      Grains of paradise
                               Annatto
                                        Juniper berries.

A keel for balance. Sturdy rudder. Slips waiting. Anchors, berths.
Finely carved figureheads in harbor—
  Medusa
        Siren
               Lady Liberty
                       Fiji Mermaid
                               Cybeles.

Signs

She had signs hanging all over her house. *God Lives Here, Bless this House, Count Your Blessings.* One over the stove, a crooked one beside the front door, a circular hanging in front of the kitchen window. I watch for signs. Red skies at night, the birds gone quiet, frog spawn for an early spring. A gelatinous clump lumped on the shallow shelf of the creek skidding along the back fence. Each day, I check it. A March month of monitoring. Alert for cotton threads signaling fungus. A death notice. Late frost. Watching for pearls to bob. Burgeon. Water boatmen watch for signs, too. Backswimmers. Ready for the push and pull of fragile forked legs. Dinner. Devouring. All the while avoiding. Alert for water scorpions. The water boatmen's death knell.

Daddy's Home

Afternoon sits at the end of my walkway. Pouts between two clumps

of monkey grass. Staring at the front door. Swats at morning

on occasion. Wants to get going before night calm commences.

The cats peer out the front window. Hiss and growl a welcome.

Ready to curl into a C and nap in the heat of 2:00 p.m.

A quick shower drops by, offers afternoon a drink.

Tells him to stand up. Be a man. Afternoon

marches up to the door and enters the quiet house.

Punches a wall. Smacks morning around some. Daddy's home.

Plum Point Park

Shark-shaped,
gobbling up the river.
Resting in the shallows.

Trails and Treks of West Ghent

The buzz of bakeries, beer trucks,
poodle groomers. Rambling walks,
wide-planked porches, trails to the
Wishing Tree. All for you and me.

Dismal Swamp @ Dusk

In daylight, a wretched mass of wet and mangled tree carcasses. Bones scratching warnings in the sky. Submerged souls, abandoned cars. At a knife past dusk, far worse.
The Great Dismal Swamp.

Teacher conferences were brutal. Criers, screamers, shoulder-shruggers. After, I began my trek home to a glass of wine and my easy chair. Then, a four-car pile-up right before my exit. I was roosting on the cusp of that black hole for a solid hour, listening to NPR, when I saw a flash out of the corner of my eye. An albino buck. Ten-point rack. Flanks quivering. A silent stomp. And behind him—

Grendel.

Slick and yet leathery. A pyramid spine and eight inches of talons on each foot. Gray as the Virginia sky, with oozing eyes. Teeth jagged, shit brown. I watched him. He watched the buck flinch and spring across four lanes of traffic of rubbernecking. No one noticed the monster. Not as he watched his prey elude him nor as he folded into his body

and collapsed into a hollow cypress. Ravenous. Silently waiting for his next target. A black bear or a bobcat family passing too close. A hitchhiker between destination and the rim of the swamp. A weary teacher changing a flat tire. Or one stuck in a traffic jam. Unfolding from her car to take a piss on the brim of the Great Dismal Swamp.

No Magnolia Wreaths

The peninsula yawns her daybreak. Boats

    thread the throat of the harbor, all under the bright eye

of the sun. Estuary stones slick and deep witness. Prehistoric fish

    sleep under the white-capped blanket. Kelp threads. Roads

traverse the land, dip, and disappear under the lip of earth, a tunnel

    to the body of the mainland. Trees, not seas,

miles beyond the reach of the awakening peninsula. Her mouth

    whispering a prayer for those bound, those tethered to dirt,

unable to crest and roll like those ruled by nothing but the whim
    of wind and wave.

No blessing of the fleet.

    No magnolia wreath.

I Come from a Long Line of Storytellers

She insisted evening lay down softly. Told us it pulled
a pillow from the sky and stretched out in Boone Valley
under the watchful eye of Storyteller's Rock. She

said this so we wouldn't worry. Didn't want us to know
the pain when dry lightning cut through evening's spine.
How when it tumbled, evening reached out to take purchase

of the loblolly and the bullbrier to break the fall. Ripping
open wrists and tearing fingers. The dark sky streaked in red.
She was silent about the jagged rocks, granite cut and sawed

by glaciers eons ago, piercing its back. But we knew of the suffering.
Evening came, but it did not gently recline. Thrashing wildly
and crashing down instead. All we could do was watch

as she smiled. A storyteller
to the end.

Title Index

A

A Gwynn Island Blessing for a Fair Sail 28
Another Hiker Lost in the Woods 59
Apple Picking During Covid 22
Ashes to Ashes 48

B

Beware of Strangers Bearing Gifts in the Garden 31
Breaking and Entering 34
Brother's Log Cabin and Equine 53
Bull Beach as My Mother Goes Blind 16

C

Charon Stops by Cedar Grove Cemetery 23
Cousin Stan Steals 52

D

Daddy's Home 62
Dismal Swamp @ Dusk 65

F

Flailing 35

G

Guardrails and Armrests 57

H

He was an out-of-work snake preacher 32

I

I cannot take a lover 29
I Come from a Long Line of Storytellers 67
If It's Not Broken 27
I Learned Silence 49
I Think of the Peonies 39

L

Like the *Mary Celeste* 38

M

Molting to More 42
My Back to the Fescue 25
My Daughter 51

N

Neap tide 47
No Magnolia Wreaths 66
Norfolk Greets Lord Dunmore 36

P

Pickett's Tomb, Hollywood Cemetery,
   Richmond, Virginia 18
Plum Point Park 63
Port Haywood 44
Pretty Bottles All in a Row 15

S

Saint Somebody Deep in Appalachia 54
Saturday Chores on Greenbrier Road 26
She Holds Book to Belly 55
Signs 61

T

The Ash-Freckled Snow 50
The Ghost Forest 46
The Hurricane 43
The Rails We Ride 58
There is nothing more graceful than
  the passage of a pregnant lady 60
the ruts of highway 58 37
The Texture of the Heart 17
This Neighborhood 40
Trails and Treks of West Ghent 64

W

We Long for Broken Waters and Full Sails 30
What He Heard in Leavenworth 19
What You Fail to See from
  Your Kitchen Window 45
When I Build My Snow Globe 41
When I Tell You This, I Lie 21
When the Fairies Take
  Residence for Winter 20
Where the Fairies Frolic 24
Winter Waits 56

First Line Index

A

Afternoon sits at the end of my walkway.
   Pouts between two clumps 62
Again, I am ten. My 25
A long weekend in a cracked cottage leaning 28

D

Dogwoods stood sentry
   under the Union blue sky 18
Down Greenbrier Street,
   a block before the estuary 35

F

for the right side of the bed,
   given to me by Great Aunt Martha 29

I

If you peel back the pericardium,
   snap the thick sac, tear 17
I have heard tales of bluebell woods 24

I have seen the silver rabbit three times now 31
I have spoken of Deltaville.
    How we cast off our kayaks 45
I have taken her items that are chipped,
    torn, water-stained. I did 27
I learned silence like braille, feeling the bumps 49
In daylight, a wretched mass of wet
    and mangled tree carcasses 65
In my snow globe, I will position
    Dad in his recliner 41
I stand on the HVAC unit outside
    the bedroom window, pull 34
I tell you that I sometimes see a
    flash of a slick segmented tail 21
I think of the peonies. Not the
    unplugging of monitors and alerts 39
It storms the coast, rears back its head,
    and roars. Sour-breath 43

L

Listen for the bells of old St. Paul 36

M

My daughter is a storm with bones of wind 51
My grandparents' home was thumb-smashed 15
My mother will tell you. And my
    grandmother, too. To clean 26

O

Our car left the valley,
    began to climb the mountains 57
Owned one dead snake and one
    with a nasty boil directly above his 32

R

    Roots. Bones. Both gnarled, white. Grasping 59

S

    Sailboats tight with anchors resist
        the change of tide like the broken 30
    Shark-shaped 63
    She had signs hanging all over her house.
        God Lives Here, Bless this 61
    She insisted evening lay down softly.
        Told us it pulled 67
    She says the new drops sting,
        the magnifying glass is no help, and 16
    She stands near to two feet,
        one palm reaching out in surrender 54
    Steel stitching nearly across the back stoop step 58

T

    The buzz of bakeries, beer trucks 64
    the couple walks the fringe 47
    The fairies in the field have
        moved to the attic. The frost-tipped nettle 20
    The marsh will walk. Stomp right 46
    The occupants of the peach-colored
        Cape Cod sitting catty-corner 55
    The paths of the water, jagged
        incomplete jigsaw puzzles. Harbors 44
    The peninsula yawns her daybreak. Boats 66
    There is nothing more graceful
        than the passage of a pregnant lady 60
    the trees were not blurred. each distinct.
        the knot holes, broken 37
    They both lorried up to the fence.

One bay, the other a pinto 53
They honored him at halftime.
   On the same emerald field 19
They say the snow will begin just after one 48
They stare at me as they slice
   their slab of Easter ham 52
This neighborhood. The dog
   behind us barks in frustration at his 40
Three streets over, at the sea-foam
   green ranch, the family car 23
Two teenagers play in the ash-freckled snow 50

W

We long to be more than just
   another tourist, what the locals call 42
We paid our fare at the bottom gate 22
Will it be like the *Flying Dutchman*
   or maybe the *Mary Celeste* 38
Winter waits. To devour.
   Feed on the unsuspecting 56

www.ingramcontent.com/pod-product-compliance
Lightning Source LLC
Chambersburg PA
CBHW010047090426
42735CB00020B/3418